IMAGES
of America

RANDOLPH FIELD

Capt. William Millican Randolph (1893–1928) was the namesake of Randolph Field. Having attended the Agricultural and Mechanical College of Texas (now Texas A&M), he entered the Army in 1916. He finished pilot training at Kelly Field in 1919, too late for World War I. He was a member of a special committee that was seeking a suitable location for the new training field. Unfortunately, Randolph was killed in the crash of his Curtiss AT-4 at Gorman, Texas, on February 17, 1928. The War Department agreed to name the new field in honor of Randolph seven months later. Captain Randolph was buried at Fort Sam Houston National Cemetery. (Courtesy of the Air Force Education and Training Command Office of History and Research.)

On the Cover: No picture of Randolph Field's iconic Administration Building, known as the "Taj Mahal," would be complete without a host of airplanes flying overhead. In this case, at least 18 North American BT-14 training planes do the honors. The huge, 48-star garrison flag adds to the effect. (Courtesy of the Air Force Education and Training Command Office of History and Research.)

IMAGES
of America

RANDOLPH FIELD

Lt. Col. Michael P. Hoffman (USAF Retired)

ARCADIA
PUBLISHING

ISBN 978-1-4671-3233-6

Published by Arcadia Publishing
Charleston, South Carolina

Printed in the United States of America

Library of Congress Control Number: 2014935199

For all general information, please contact Arcadia Publishing:
Telephone 843-853-2070
Fax 843-853-0044
E-mail sales@arcadiapublishing.com
For customer service and orders:
Toll-Free 1-888-313-2665

Visit us on the Internet at www.arcadiapublishing.com

To my father, Lt. Col. Charles L. Hoffman Jr. (USAF-Ret.), and mother, Georgia Papageorge Hoffman, members of "the Greatest Generation;" and to my wife, Kay Kirklin Hoffman, who put up with all the time I spent at the computer keyboard.

Contents

ACKNOWLEDGMENTS

The beauty of the buildings on Randolph Field and its unique shape made it a well-photographed subject.

The author would like to acknowledge the assistance of the staff of the Air Force Education and Training Command (AETC) Office of History and Research, especially command historian Gary D. Boyd and art program and museum curator Robert V. Crawford. Their cooperation in allowing me access to their archives was essential to the compilation of this book.

All photographs herein are from the United States Air Force, courtesy of the AETC Office of History and Research.

Introduction

On a flat tract of former farmland about 17 miles northeast of downtown San Antonio, Texas, the Army Corps of Engineers, in its biggest project since the Panama Canal, built in fewer than three years a permanent airfield that resembled a Spanish village. That airfield was known as Randolph Field from its dedication in 1930 until the Air Force became a separate service in 1947 and retitled its installations as "Air Force Bases." By the mid-1930s, Randolph Field's fame had spread, and it was known as the "West Point of the Air" since the Army Air Corps had no national military academy devoted solely to producing aviators. Because of its architectural beauty, Randolph is now called the "Showplace of the Air Force."

Randolph Field's roots were planted in controversy. After the loss of the Navy dirigible USS *Shenandoah* in 1925, outspoken Air Service general William "Billy" Mitchell accused Army and Navy leadership of "almost treasonable administration of the national defense." As he was already a thorn in the side of Pres. Calvin Coolidge, the president ordered Mitchell to be court-martialed. Mitchell used the resulting trial as a sounding board for championing military aviation and criticizing military leadership. He was convicted and sentenced to suspension for five years without pay, which Coolidge later adjusted to half pay. Mitchell resigned instead.

So much public criticism arose over the state of military aviation during this period that Coolidge appointed a board to look at the issue and make recommendations. Called the Morrow Board because of Dwight D. Morrow's chairmanship, the panel made recommendations that led to the US Army Air Corps Act of 1926. One of the results of that act was that the Air Service became the Army Air Corps on July 2, 1926. A major part of the act was the authorization for the Air Corps to begin a five-year expansion program that would begin July 1, 1927. The goal was for the Air Corps to reach 1,800 airplanes, 1,650 officers, and 15,000 enlisted men by mid-1932.

At the time of the Air Corps Act, flying training was conducted at Brooks and Kelly Fields, on the southeast and west sides, respectively, of San Antonio. Brooks conducted primary and basic flying training, and Kelly had advanced flying training. The commander of the newly designated Air Corps Training Center was Brig. Gen. Frank P. Lahm, one of the Army's original two pilots. Lahm was tasked to make recommendations on what the Air Corps would have to do to increase its output of pilots.

At first, it was assumed that Brooks and Kelly Fields could handle the increase, but Lahm soon discovered that there was not enough operating room at the two bases to handle the load. Consequently, he began looking for a location for a new airfield that could handle all primary, basic, and advanced flying training. Various sites were scouted out around San Antonio and even in other parts of Texas. When the word got back to San Antonio leaders, however, they became worried that the new airfield, if built elsewhere, would lessen the importance of Brooks and Kelly and might even lead to closures. So, city leaders worked to not only find a location near San Antonio, but also to help purchase the land and "give" it to the Air Corps, if it would build the airfield there.

Lahm finally settled on 2,319 acres of farmland in northeast Bexar County near Cibolo Creek, located on State Highway 3 between the two little towns of Converse and Schertz. City leaders formed the San Antonio Airport Company to buy options on the needed land, and eventually two dozen farms were purchased for $546,000. On August 18, 1928, the War Department accepted San Antonio's gift.

Now that land had been procured, it was time to design an airfield. Lt. Harold L. Clark, who was a motor pool officer at Kelly Field but had architecture training, became intrigued by the idea of a new, permanent airfield (no temporary wooden buildings) and began sketching out ideas of how he thought this "Air City" should look. He came up with the idea that the buildings should have a Spanish Colonial Revival style. It was proposed that the airfield should be square in shape, with three sides devoted to the three phases of flying training: primary, basic, and advanced. After much debate, it was also decided that all living quarters would be inside the square, with officers' quarters in a circle within the square. To provide a centerpiece for this airfield, Clark designed an administration building with a tall tower. This building, after some modifications, became known as the "Taj Mahal" because of its Spanish, Art Deco, and Moorish features. Clark showed his ideas to another officer, who immediately wanted to show them to General Lahm. Lahm was so impressed by the plans that he put Clark on his staff, and Clark began to design the "Air City." Later, Clark was assigned to the chief of the Air Corps, where he continued his work.

Construction on the future Randolph Field began in the spring of 1929 with the clearing of the farmland. The road system was laid out, and a spur from the nearby railroad was built to bring in building materials. There were underground utilities for power and communications. In November 1929, construction began on the first two buildings, which were warehouses. The construction of four enlisted barracks closely followed. On June 30, 1930, the partially completed airfield was dedicated and named after Capt. William M. Randolph, who had been killed in an airplane accident on February 17, 1928.

Construction continued on officer and noncommissioned officer (NCO) quarters, bachelor officer quarters, additional enlisted barracks, a cadet area, various maintenance and administrative buildings, a motor pool, a Post Exchange, a Post School, a hospital, a building for the School of Aviation Medicine, officer and NCO clubs, four swimming pools, and 18 hangars. By October 1931 most construction was completed, and training began on November 2 of that year.

Over the next 10 years, thousands of officers and aviation cadets would enter the gates of Randolph Field and depart as pilots. It turned out that only primary and basic training could be accommodated at Randolph, so advanced flying training remained at Kelly. It was during this time that Randolph became known as the "West Point of the Air." A movie by that title was even filmed and released in the mid-1930s.

Because of the plethora of interesting photographs taken in the 1920s and 1930s, this book is solely devoted to Randolph Field from the beginning of construction in 1928 up to America's entry into World War II in 1941.

One

The Air Corps Training Center

Brig. Gen. Frank P. Lahm (1877–1963), seen here as a major general, was generally regarded as the "Father of Randolph Field." It was Lahm who selected the site for Randolph, approved the basic layout, and oversaw the construction. One of the first two military aviators trained by the Wright brothers in 1909, Lahm had a long career in aviation and was commanding officer of the Air Corps Training Center when construction began at Randolph. He retired on November 20, 1941. After his death, he was cremated and his ashes were spread over Randolph Air Force Base.

This February 8, 1928, photograph looking west shows the farmland that would become Randolph Field. The white area in the upper center was about where the west flight line would be. In the foreground was the town of Schertz. The diagonal slash from lower left to middle right was the Galveston, Houston & San Antonio Railroad (now Union Pacific), paralleled by State Highway 3 (now Farm to Market Road 78).

This was the view from the west toward the site of the future Randolph Field, also taken on February 2, 1928. The diagonal from middle left to lower right was the railroad and State Highway 3. The road coming in from the middle right was Kneupper Road, now overlaid by Loop 1604. The town of Converse was out of frame to the right.

This was downtown San Antonio on February 21, 1929. The site of Randolph Field was the thin, light area in the upper right center, just below the horizon. Fort Sam Houston was around the large light area at the upper right.

This is a February 12, 1928, vertical view of the area where Randolph Field would be constructed. The "x" marks the approximate center of the installation, where the Officers' Club would be located. The curving line in the upper right was Cibolo Creek. The horizontal road across the bottom of the photograph was, and still is, Lower Seguin Road.

Lt. Harold L. Clark (1893–1973), then a dispatch officer at the Kelly Field motor pool, was the creator of the original layout of Randolph Field. Having heard of a new airfield to be built that would accommodate all three phases of flying training—primary, basic, and advanced—he came up with the idea of having runways on three sides of the base, hence the square shape with a circular interior. He also designed the buildings on the new field to be in the Spanish Colonial Revival style. He presented his proposal to General Lahm's executive officer, who promptly referred them to his boss. Lahm liked the plans and assigned Clark to his office to devote his full energies to designing Randolph Field. Clark retired in 1946 as a brigadier general.

Two

Construction of Randolph Field

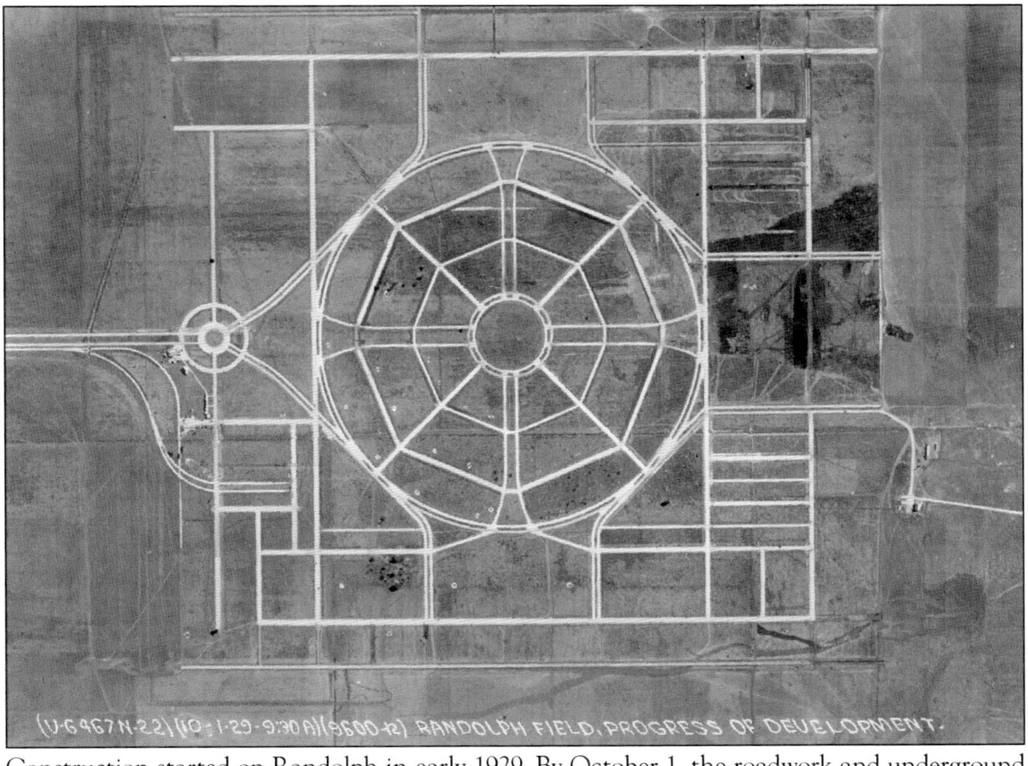

Construction started on Randolph in early 1929. By October 1, the roadwork and underground utilities were finished. The roads were not paved, but remained crushed gravel until after construction was complete, when they became concrete. The circle-within-a-square plan form was evident. Officer quarters were inside the Main Circle. Most noncommissioned officer (NCO) quarters would be at the upper right and lower right of the square. The cadet area would be in the dark square at the right side of the plan. A total of 18 hangars would line the top and bottom of the square. The shops would be located at the lower left. Bachelor officers' quarters would be at the upper left. Six enlisted barracks would be near the two rows of hangars—two at the top and four at the bottom.

This January 16, 1930, photograph shows the roads, the temporary contractor buildings, and the foundation excavations for the first permanent structures. The dark rectangles at the top were the beginnings of four enlisted barracks. Just below the string of boxcars in the upper right were the foundations for two warehouses. These six buildings would eventually become Randolph's first completed structures.

The first two buildings started and finished on Randolph were the Air Corps Supply Warehouse (left) and the Quartermaster (QM) Warehouse (right). This May 7, 1930, photograph shows that progress on the QM Warehouse was slightly ahead of its twin. Subsequent photographs seem to prove that the QM Warehouse was the oldest building on Randolph, although both buildings were accepted on the same day, November 1, 1930.

Construction on the Air Corps Shops (lower left center) was well underway when this photograph was taken on October 15, 1930. Above the shops were three buildings already completed: the small, white Guard House, the Air Corps Supply Warehouse, and the QM Warehouse. At the lower right was a finished enlisted barracks. At the bottom of the photograph were the foundations for (from left to right) Hangars J, I, and H.

Construction began on the first two enlisted barracks in late 1929. This February 5, 1930, photograph shows foundation progress on Buildings 3 and 4, on the west side of Randolph Field. Note the temporary railroad spur that brought in construction material. In the distance was the foundation work on the Air Corps Supply Warehouse and the QM Warehouse. The town of Schertz was in the right distance.

By June 17, 1930, the west-side enlisted barracks were progressing. Behind them, the two warehouses were almost finished. In the 1960s, Building 3 (left) and Building 4 (center) would be connected into one structure that would house the Air Force Military Personnel Center (now the Air Force Personnel Center). In the 1970s, Building 5 (right) would become the home of the Air Force Recruiting Service, which it still is today.

What a difference a few months make! This November 4, 1930, photograph shows four completed enlisted barracks (upper middle left), nearly finished married NCO duplexes (center and right foreground), and completed warehouses and Air Corps Shops (beyond the barracks). At the upper right, some married officers' quarters were completed, while others were under construction. At left were the foundations for hangars and a nearly completed Operations and Parachute Building.

Construction of the east enlisted barracks was behind that of the west. In this November 4, 1930, photograph, Building 7 (top) was almost complete, while Building 8 (bottom) was still having structural concrete poured. Currently, Building 7 (now Building 399) houses base-level functions such as finance, military and civilian personnel, and traffic management. Building 8 (now Building 581) is occupied by Air Education and Training Command (AETC) logistics, installations, and mission support functions.

This December 15, 1930, photograph shows construction on the west flight line. The West Operations Office (lower left center) was complete. Hangars F (left) and E (right) flanked it. Hangar F would become the base gymnasium. The enlisted barracks across the street were also completed. From this photograph, it is clear that the construction of officer housing on the west side was ahead of that on the east side.

Construction on the east flight line was well under way by December 15, 1930. At the bottom center of this photograph was the East Operations Office, flanked by the skeletal beginnings of Hangars P (left) and O (right). Across the street from the Operations Office was the future site of one of the base's four swimming pools, or "Auxiliary Water Storage Tanks," as they were officially known. The two east-side enlisted barracks were complete (right) and nearly complete (left).

By December 15, 1930, the 38 NCO duplexes on the southwest corner of Randolph were nearing completion. In the lower center of this photograph, the foundation work on the Station Hospital was underway. Officers' quarters in the circle were progressing well, as was the Officers' Club. The hangars on the east flight line had their steel framework up but were not complete.

The circular road in the middle of Randolph was named Military Plaza. Here, Military Plaza waited empty on June 17, 1930, for the builders to begin construction on the Officers' Club. Construction of only a few of the officers' quarters had begun. In the center right, the two warehouses were nearing completion. The enlisted barracks at the center left were well underway.

By November 17, 1930, the framework for the Officers' Club was mostly completed, and the filling in with clay tile had begun. Only a few of the officers' quarters were completed or nearing completion. In the distance, warehouses, shops, enlisted barracks, and other support facilities were finished and being used. Less than a year later, Randolph Field would be operational.

By mid-December 1930, construction was progressing on the Administration Building ("Taj Mahal"), and the Air Corps star in Washington Circle (lower left) was starting to fill in. In the lower center, the Post Exchange foundation was being laid. At the center left, the foundation of Building A of the Bachelor Officers' Quarters was underway. Also at center left, the Fire Station was complete. At upper left, most of the officers' quarters were just foundations, although a few were complete or almost complete. At the center top, the two enlisted barracks were complete or nearing completion. Five NCO duplexes just above the Bachelor Officers' Quarters were under construction.

A year after construction started, only a few of the many buildings projected to be built were completed.

This photograph shows the Taj Mahal under construction on May 17, 1931. Note the 500,000-gallon water tank being erected inside the building. Officers' and married NCOs' quarters were mostly completed. At the top, enlisted barracks, west flight line hangars, and the Operations and Parachute Building were completed. The grassy area in the foreground would be the site of the Post Chapel in 1934.

By June 24, 1931, Randolph was nearly complete. The Taj Mahal, at right, still had scaffolding around the tower, and there were a few officers' quarters under construction at upper left. In the foreground were the two U-shaped Bachelor Officers' Quarters flanking the mess (dining hall). Note that the Air Corps labeled this photograph as "Hospital," even though the hospital was barely discernible on the opposite, far side of the base.

The Post Exchange was also complete by June 24, 1931, although the little Gas Station at the right of the exchange was still under construction. Sharing the same block as the exchange was the Fire Station. Across the road from the exchange were the Post Garage, the QM Maintenance Building (center right), and the QM Warehouses. At this point, most of the other buildings within view were complete.

This November 17, 1930, photograph shows the Academic Building (lower center), in the cadet area, structurally complete but still unfinished. To the left and right were the foundations for Cadet Barracks A and B. Note that there were still vacant lots and unfinished houses in the officers' quarters' area.

At the time of this December 5, 1930, photograph, the Academic Building (lower center) was nearing completion, construction had begun on Cadet Barracks B (right of Academic Building), and foundations were laid for the Cadet Administration Building (below Academic Building) and Cadet Barracks A (left of Academic Building).

This no-nonsense-looking officer was Maj. Harrison H.C. Richards (1890–1951), commander of Randolph Field during its construction. He would give way to Maj. Frederick L. Martin in October 1931. He retired as a colonel in 1947.

Mrs. William M. Randolph, the lady in white, officiated the raising of the flag, thus dedicating Randolph Field in her husband's honor on June 20, 1930. Brig. Gen. Frank P. Lahm was to Mrs. Randolph's left and slightly behind. Other dignitaries present were Mayor C.M. Chambers of San Antonio and Maj. Gen. James E. Fechet, chief of the Air Corps.

The flag-raising ceremonies occurred when Randolph's construction had barely begun—note the uncompleted enlisted barracks in the background. Here, Mrs. Randolph had raised Old Glory to the top of a makeshift flagpole on the west side of the base.

The grand finale of Randolph's dedication was a spectacular flyby of 233 airplanes from Brooks and Kelly Fields, Fort Crockett (Galveston), and Fort Sill, Oklahoma. Described as "the largest assembly of aircraft in the world," this was probably not hyperbole, as post–World War I national aviation budgets had been slashed. Here, nine biplane bombers (Martin NBS-1s from Kelly Field) lumbered past the reviewing stand and crowd of over 15,000 people.

These were contractors who built Randolph. They did a magnificent job of constructing an operational airfield from farmland in fewer than three years. The contractors posed at the entrance of one of the warehouses.

Three

"West Point of the Air"

Maj. Frederick L. Martin (1882–1954) was commanding officer of Randolph Field when it became operational in October 1931. The first class, with 210 officers and 99 cadets, began training on November 2, 1931. Martin remained commander until July 7, 1934. He achieved early fame when he was commander of the Army's around-the-world flight of 1924. As commander of the Hawaiian Air Force in 1941, he bore some of the blame for the Pearl Harbor debacle. Martin retired as a major general in 1944.

This November 17, 1931, photograph shows mostly finished Randolph Field. Later, land would be annexed in the upper right and at the bottom. During World War II, a south ramp was added and concrete runways replaced grass on the left and right flight lines. The very bottom would become a golf course in the late 1940s. The areas to the left and right of the entrance drive at the top (now Harmon Drive) would fill with Wherry housing for officers and airmen in the early 1950s. This housing would be razed in the 2000s, and the area returned to parkland. The checkerboard area at the very top of the photograph was the beginnings of Universal City, a speculative land development project that would not see fruition until the late 1950s. Schertz was at the upper right.

When finished, this magnificent building was known simply as Building 100, or the Administration Building. Its Spanish Colonial Revival style, with Moorish and Art Deco overtones, led to the nickname of "Taj Mahal," or simply "the Taj." Built at a cost of $252,000, the Taj housed the offices of the commanding general of the Air Corps Training Center and the commanding officer of Randolph Field. Also in the building were the signal office, provost marshal, personnel, finance, recruiting, post office, telegraph office, print shop, photographic section, and public relations. The 170-foot octagonal tower served a function; it enclosed a 500,000-gallon water tank. In the rear of the building was a 1,150-seat movie theater/auditorium. The space beneath the dome originally served as a weather office, but is now vacant. The building is currently the headquarters for the 12th Flying Training Wing.

This unusual angle shows the cruciform shape of the Taj Mahal. The long projection to the upper right was the movie theater/auditorium. The "Randolph Field" lettering in front was in place before the building was even begun, and still exists today.

The main entrance to the Taj Mahal was impressive, especially to newly arriving cadets. At the right was the Post Garage.

At the rear of the Taj Mahal was the post theater. The interior of the theater has not changed much through the years.

This was a pilot's eye view of the Taj Mahal, as seen from the cockpit of a training plane, possibly a Fairchild PT-19 "Cornell."

This early 1932 photograph shows the north-south axis of Randolph. The Commanding General's Quarters were at the end of the boulevard, above the Officers' Club. At the top of the photograph were the Taj Mahal (center), the Fire Station and Post Exchange (left), and Bachelor Officers' Quarters A (right). At the very top was the faint outline of Randolph Boulevard, part of which would later become today's Pat Booker Road.

On the far east side of Randolph was Lt. Norfleet G. Bone's hothouse and nursery for landscaping plants. To the right is the road (now Texas Farm to Market Road 1518) that paralleled Cibolo Creek. The hothouse and nursery no longer exist, but the area is still used for recreational purposes. The excavated area to the right became the site of Randolph's water treatment plant, which was later abandoned.

Even in the 1930s, the Air Corps practiced xeriscaping. Considering the long, hot Texas summers and the propensity for droughts, Lieutenant Bone planted this combination of cacti, rocks, and drought-resistant shrubs in the main circle median. Unfortunately, this did not last, and the more attractive and water-thirsty grass eventually replaced the cacti. The structure at the far right was Bachelor Officers' Quarters A.

The Officers' Club was built in the same Spanish Colonial Revival style as the rest of the base. The club has been greatly expanded since its original, simple, two-story design. The arched entrance still exists, but is inside the building now. A ballroom extension completed around 1953 filled in the area at the left. The circular driveway was relocated to the right.

This is the reverse (south) side of the Officers' Club. Like the north side, this face of the club was considerably altered. The upstairs balcony and the lower arcade were enclosed and the club was widened in the late 1950s to increase the interior floor space. This photograph is undated, but it appears to have been taken on November 20, 1931.

The first floor of the Officers' Club served as the reception room. Except for some cosmetic changes and upgrades in furniture, this part of the club is mostly unchanged. Even the barely discernible fireplace at left still exists.

In 1932, the second floor of the Officers' Club served as a ballroom. This room has changed little except for an expansion that enclosed the balcony outside of the curtained windows at right. The exposed rafters are no longer visible.

The Officers' Club patio offered respite from the hot Texas sun. This area has been closed off and is now part of the interior of the club.

Across from the patio at the rear of the Officers' Club was the magnificent pool and bathhouse. There were two "kiddie" pools, at the left and right sides of the main pool. Also, note the lack of fences in those simple, carefree days. At the time of this photograph, May 25, 1932, Randolph's landscaping was only beginning. The pool is still operating today.

The Air Corps photographer hit a home run with the composition of this photograph. The centerpiece of the Officers' Club pool was the combination high-dive platform and two lower-level diving boards. The platform was removed in the late 1970s or early 1980s due to safety concerns.

The bachelor officers' area had two U-shaped apartment buildings (Building A, to the left, and Building B, to the right) and an open mess in the center. The eight rectangular buildings in front were automobile garages that were later razed, replaced by a static display of training airplanes. The five buildings around the semicircular drive in the foreground were married NCO duplexes. In the lower left were married officers' quarters.

In the two-story front section of the Bachelor Officers' Mess were a lounge, a reception area, seven rooms for visiting officers, and a library. The connecting section was the mess. A roof garden over the mess hall was used for social functions. The rear section featured the kitchen and small rooms with a common bathroom for workers. This building now houses Force Support Squadron offices.

Again proving that Air Corps photographers were no amateurs, this was an especially well-composed view of the lawn in front of one of the Bachelor Officers' Quarters, as seen through one of the arched openings of the loggia.

The interior of the Bachelor Officers' Mess was spartan, but perhaps befitting for Air Corps officers of the 1930s. Today, this area has been partitioned into office space for the Force Support Squadron.

This cozy setup was the interior of one of the 40 apartments in each of the Bachelor Officers' Quarters' buildings. An apartment consisted of a parlor, a bedroom, a closet, and a small bathroom. The fireplace at the right was probably useful only a few days out of the year in the balmy South Texas winters. There were no kitchens, since the officers were expected to dine in the adjacent Bachelor Officers' Mess.

This is an aerial perspective of the Station Hospital (center left) and its environs. To the right of the hospital was the School of Aviation Medicine. Officers' quarters were at the lower right. In the upper third of the photograph were NCO duplexes, garages, and the West NCO Club. Across the top were Hangars C, D, and E, and to the west were the Operations and Parachute Building and an enlisted barracks.

The Station Hospital was composed of three sections. The front section contained administrative offices and a dental clinic. The middle section contained medical and surgical wards, the operating room, the clinical laboratory, and the sick call room. In the rear were the obstetrical ward, a cadet ward, another medical ward, and the mess hall and kitchens.

This 1935 photograph shows the ornate facade of the Station Hospital. The Randolph Field Historic District documentation described the entrance as "flanked by cast-stone surround with paired corkscrew columns and full entablature." The facility had a capacity of 200 beds. It served as the base's hospital until the new clinic opened in June 1989. Today, the building provides office space for several AETC major staff agencies.

This sparsely furnished area was the Station Hospital recreation room.

"Utilitarian" would probably be a good adjective to describe the Station Hospital's kitchen and serving area. Of course, during the Great Depression, any meal was greatly appreciated.

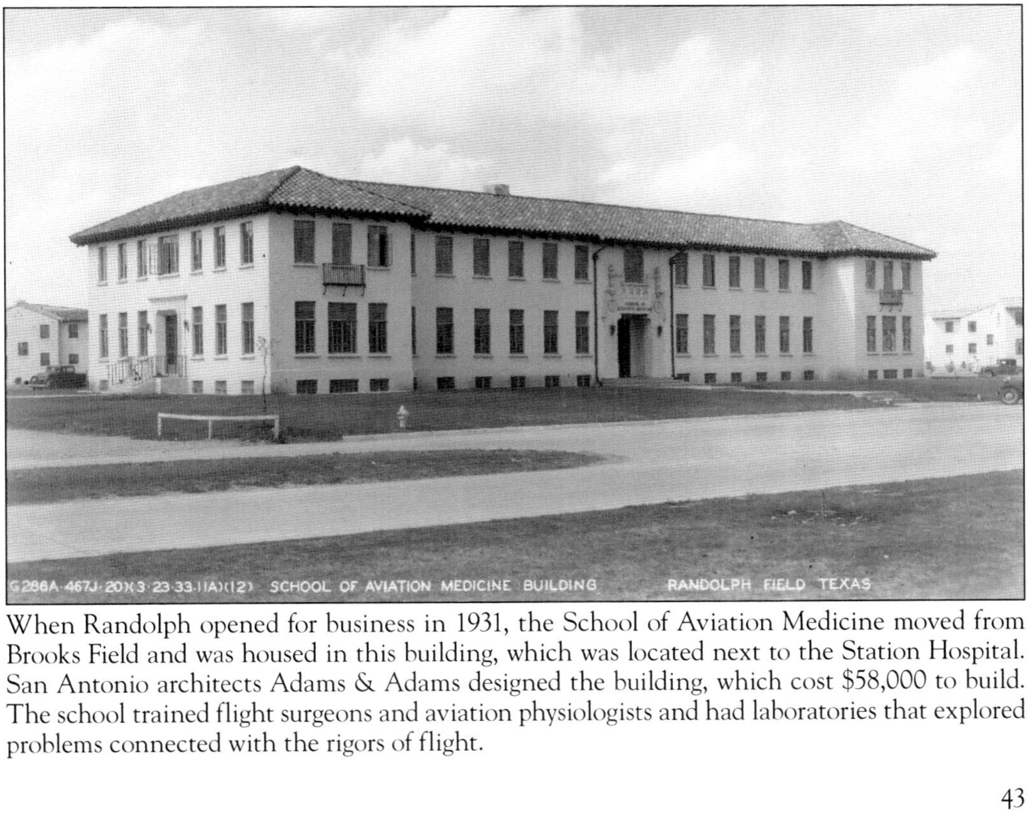

When Randolph opened for business in 1931, the School of Aviation Medicine moved from Brooks Field and was housed in this building, which was located next to the Station Hospital. San Antonio architects Adams & Adams designed the building, which cost $58,000 to build. The school trained flight surgeons and aviation physiologists and had laboratories that explored problems connected with the rigors of flight.

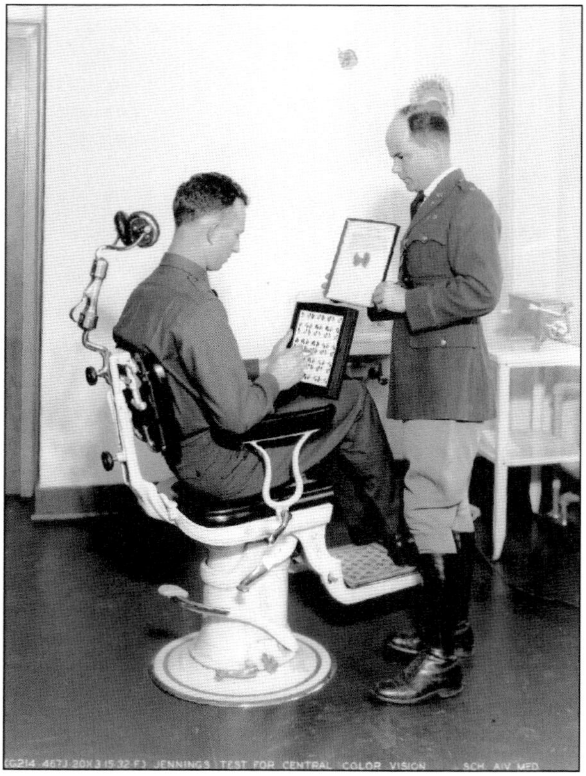

"Shave and a haircut, please!" No, this was not a barber's chair. This person—a cadet "guinea pig" perhaps—was undergoing a Jennings test for color vision in the School of Aviation Medicine.

This lieutenant had not found a new way to meet girls. He was being given a "Complex Co-ordinator Test" in the School of Aviation Medicine, which appeared to be a rudimentary test of coordination and flying capability.

The cadet area featured Barracks A (left), the Academic Building (center), and Barracks B (right). Below the Academic Building was the Cadet Administration Building, and below it was the cadet pool and bathhouse. The spaces to the left and right of the Administration Building were used for calisthenics and military drill. These buildings became Air Training Command (ATC) offices in 1957. The pool is still in use.

The Cadet Academic Building, designed by San Antonio architect Ralph Cameron, was one of the more ornamental structures on Randolph Field. Finished at a cost of $151,000 and built in a Spanish Renaissance Revival style, the entrance to the building featured "an elaborate portico cast-stone surround with a cartouche." This June 8, 1934, photograph shows how the landscapers transformed what had been featureless farmer's fields just five years earlier.

One of the classes conducted in the Academic Building was this Morse code course taught by Lt. Benjamin J. Cabell (rear). The cadets would hear code transmitted through their headphones and would have to write down what they heard. This was not a class for the hard of hearing.

Another important class was meteorology. It was important for cadets to understand weather phenomena and be able to read meteorology maps. Woe be unto the pilot who took off without knowing what weather he would encounter along his flight path. Aviation cadets attended ground school classes in this building for 20 years before Headquarters, Crew Training Air Force, took over in 1952.

This was the technical library in the second-floor west wing of the Academic Building. Through the windows, the Cadet Administration Building (left) and Cadet Barracks A (right) are visible. In 1957, the ATC (now AETC) commander and his immediate staff moved their offices into the building, and have been there ever since.

The cadet mess hall was located in the center of the Administration Building. Below the upper windows were six panoramic murals depicting cadet life, painted in the early 1940s by artist William Dean Fausett. Unfortunately, when the mess hall was converted to office space and the murals were taken down, five panels were lost. The AETC command conference room now occupies this space.

It was chow time, and the cadets enjoyed a meal in the mess hall. This photograph was taken before the Fausett murals graced the upper walls. The map of the United States in the rear of the mess hall still exists, but it is covered by a false wall.

Although not of the greatest quality, this photograph shows cadets in the library on the second floor of the Administration Building. Other than the piano in the back, there did not appear to be any other mechanical devices for entertainment. How did they get by in those days?

When Randolph was first constructed, there were only two cadet barracks, both designed by San Antonio architect Emmett T. Jackson. This one, Barracks B (now Building 902), was located east of the Academic Building. Costing about $132,000 each, the barracks featured three stories, a full basement, 54 two-man rooms, and orderly and recreation rooms.

This was a typical cadet room. At the left were the closets and the washbasin. The door at left center opened onto a cloister-like open stoop, or veranda, that overlooked the drill field. Behind the photographer was another door to an enclosed hallway. Furniture consisted of two cots, two chairs, and two desks. Later, as the number of cadets in training increased, bunk beds for four cadets made things really cozy.

Each cadet room had two built-in closets and a washbasin. Showers and toilets were down the hall. There was a proper place for everything in the closet and the drawers, and inspectors homed in on any infractions. Infractions led to demerits, and demerits could lead to walking "tours" (marching back and forth by oneself on the drill field) instead of joining one's buddies on a weekend pass.

This was the enclosed hallway of a cadet barracks. Across from the large windows at left, there was another set of windows for each cadet room, probably to facilitate cross-ventilation. The hallway allowed the cadets some privacy as they went from their rooms to the showers and toilets. Two more identical barracks were constructed in 1939 for $169,000 each.

There was nothing like a fresh dip in the cadet pool to wash away the aches and pains of marching and flying in the Texas heat. Located on the very southern part of Randolph, the pool and bathhouse were popular with the cadets, as this photograph attests. This pool is still in use today, as one of the remaining two pools out of the four originally constructed.

By the time of this November 30, 1932, photograph, the Air Corps Shops (also known as the Engineering Shops) were humming away, maintaining engines and repairing airframes that were too heavy or too complicated for hangar crews. This was the anchor facility in the industrial part of Randolph. Today, the 12th Flying Training Wing's maintenance director still uses the building.

This was the impressive main entrance to the central wing of the Air Corps Shops. The Randolph Field Historic District described the central wing as having "a recessed, rounded arch entrance and cast-stone surround with radiating voussoirs."

The east flying area was called B Stage, because it was where the basic flying training took place. Basic was the second of the three stages of the Air Corps flying training program. This January 4, 1932, photograph shows training planes lined up on the turf. The hangars were lettered from K, at top, to R, at the bottom.

These were the interiors of Hangars M, L, and K, on the east flight line, in August 1932. With the small size of the airplanes of that era, most of Randolph's complement of aircraft could be accommodated inside the spacious hangars. Today, many of Randolph's hangars are no longer used to harbor airplanes; they are now office space, and the planes are kept under canopies on the parking ramp.

This was the East Operations Office on July 24, 1935. Later, this would become known as Base Operations, where most dignitaries were received. The structure to the left held spotlights to illuminate night operations. Later, the little radio control tower cupola on the roof was enlarged to a full-size operations tower. This building was razed in 2000, and a new Base Operations was constructed in its place.

This is a 1943 photograph of the rear (west) side of the East Operations Office. The two-story raised part of the building closest to the camera was the parachute loft. Also, note that a larger operations tower had already replaced the smaller cupola on the roof.

Randolph's 18 hangars with Art Deco features were identical when first built. There were lean-to annexes on the flight side of the hangars. Today, most of these hangars have been converted to office space, and few have the capability to house airplanes anymore. This particular structure was Hangar Q (now Hangar 13), on the east flight line.

This is the interior of the parachute loft of one of the two operations offices at Randolph Field.

Open for operations by December 21, 1931, the west (A Stage) flight line conducted primary flying training with Consolidated PT-1s and PT-3s. Those were paved aprons in front of the hangars. The hangars ran from C, at the top, to J, at the bottom. Even today, the area at the top of the photograph is still largely rural, although some construction is beginning to creep in from the right.

The West Operations Office, also known as Building 133 (now Building 66), was virtually identical to the East Operations Office, except that it did not have an office over the jutting front of the building. Its radio control tower cupola was also replaced with a larger operations tower. It has gone through several uses and now houses the Gaylor Airman Leadership School.

The Post Exchange was one of the more unique and picturesque buildings on Randolph. This view shows the three wings with a central courtyard. The closest wing held a café, which was open to all the field's personnel, and a barbershop. The wing to the left was the grocery, meat market, and tailor shop, and the one to the right was the general store. Immediately behind the Post Exchange were the auto service area, with five bays (left), and the Gas Station. The exchange served Randolph customers until a new exchange opened in 1977. After the exchange moved out, the Class Six Store (alcoholic beverages) moved into the area where the café was originally, staying until the new BXtra Building opened in April 1999. Since then, the whole building has been used as office space for various base activities.

The Randolph Field photographer took pains composing this photograph of the Post Exchange courtyard patio and fountain. The post restaurant was through the door straight ahead. Sometime after this photograph was taken, double-tier basins were added to the center of the fountain.

This view of the Post Exchange courtyard patio shows the Quartermaster Filling Station (left) and the Gas Station (right) through the archways. At the left was the entrance to the general store wing of the exchange. The view through the arches is not possible today because of an addition that closed off that part of the building.

The Gas Station sold Esso and Humble gasoline to Randolph personnel. Decorative cement columns that resembled logs supported the overhang. The service terminated when a much larger station opened nearby in the mid-1950s. Through the years, the building was used for different things, including a shoppette (icehouse) for beer and snacks in the 1970s. It now houses the offices of the American Federation of Government Employees Local 1840.

This photograph gives a better view of the decorative cement "logs" that supported the overhang of the Post Exchange Gas Station. In 1960, the drive-through bay was filled in.

Being in a rural area, Randolph needed a school for its children. Finished in 1933, the Post School had two classroom wings that exited onto an open arcade. The center section held administrative offices. When a new school opened in 1952, this building became the Base Library. In 2003 the library moved, and the former Post School building now serves as part of the Youth Center.

This was the QM Warehouse in 1943. Originally Building 1, it now has the number 220. This building later became the Commissary, operating until September 1980, when a new Commissary opened. About one-third of the old Commissary was razed to provide room for the new Commissary. The building currently houses offices and the base post office.

This was the Air Corps Supply Warehouse, also in 1943. The building, once Building 2, is now numbered 224. It still functions as a warehouse.

The QM Maintenance Building was one of the few large original structures on Randolph that was later razed in the interest of progress. Located between the Post Garage and the QM Warehouse, its space was needed for the delivery truck loading area behind the new Commissary. Consequently, it was razed in 1978.

This forbidding Dope Storage Building stored very flammable airplane fabric lacquer (dope). After planes were no longer fabric-covered, the building was used for other purposes. It was the Class Six Store in the 1970s, then held Base Exchange offices, and is now the Security Forces' Reports and Administration Section. This building was not a place for the claustrophobic, as it had only one door and just slits for windows.

Across the street from the Dope Storage Building was the Paint and Dope Shop. This was where the paint and dope were actually applied to the airplane parts (wings, fuselage, and tail). This building still serves in its original capacity, only now it is called "Corrosion Control."

This was half of two identical buildings together known as the Engine Test Building. The other building is out of frame to the right. Inside, aircraft engines were bolted to stands and tested after undergoing maintenance. As engines grew more powerful and later became jets, these buildings were no longer needed; hence, the road between them was walled off and the area converted into a storage facility.

The Post Garage was where Randolph's government vehicles were stored and maintained. The front facade was notable for the ornate grillwork around the windows. The tower rising from the rear of the building supported a siren. The building was converted into office space and classrooms and now houses the Education Center. A portion of the rear of the building was razed in 1978 when construction of the new Commissary began.

A proud medical officer poses with his late 1920s Studebaker ambulance in front of the ornate entrance to the Post Garage.

The Post Bakery was located between the Post Garage and the QM Warehouse. It provided baked goods that could not be prepared in the various mess halls around Randolph. When the mess halls were consolidated, the bakery was no longer necessary, and the building became office space. It has now served for several years as the base veterinary office.

This small, oddly shaped building was the Electric and Gas Building, where the utility lines entered Randolph. Located across from the Post Exchange and later hidden by shrubbery, it could be easily overlooked by passersby. The building still exists, housing the offices for the Air Force Reserve Officers Training Corps' Southwest Region headquarters.

Baseball games were played at Grater Field, located near the cadet area. Cadet Barracks C (now Building 907) was at far left. NCO duplexes were behind the Grater Field stands and to the right. The stands became unsafe and were razed in the 1970s. Perhaps reflecting the times, the field was recently converted into a football and soccer field surrounded by a quarter-mile track.

Normally, something as mundane as a pump house for the sprinkler system would not be in a publication such as this, but the adjoining water tank was unique because of its crenellated top. These structures were behind (east of) the West Operations Office and lasted into the 1980s.

The Guard House was where the military police were accommodated. Inside was a cell block in which to keep miscreants, a guard dormitory, a guardroom, two small cells, an office, toilets for the guards and prisoners, and a large storage room. The arch bays in the front were later enclosed and the cell block converted to office space. The building still serves in that capacity today, as the home of Randolph's Security Forces.

The word "remote" comes to mind when viewing this photograph of the Main Gate (at the time appropriately named Outpost No. 1) of Randolph. When cadets arrived at the railroad station, which was behind and to the right of the position from which this photograph was taken, this was their first sight of Randolph Field.

This photograph, taken on February 19, 1931, shows the Main Gate and its stalwart guard. The building was just large enough for a small office and a bathroom. Lieutenant Bone's outfit had already nicely landscaped the grounds. The gate house, which was expanded with glassed-in wings in the 1950s, lasted until the 1990s, when it was razed for a larger building, which was in turn razed for the current structure.

There were two NCO clubs, each having dining areas, a reading room, a library, and a kitchen. The East NCO Club was for married NCOs, and the West NCO Club for unmarried. The east club became the sole NCO Club when the west club became the Service (Airman's) Club. A new NCO Club opened in 2003, so the old club became the Base Library. The Airman's Club is now the Airman and Family Readiness Center.

One of the earliest buildings completed at Randolph Field was the Fire Station. This February 18, 1931, photograph shows the station amidst uncompleted structures. This building served as the Fire Station until the 1960s, when a new, larger facility was built in the southeast quadrant of the base. A laundry and cleaning establishment occupied the building for several years, followed by the Office of Special Investigations detachment, and now Security Forces Training.

This July 1936 view from the top of the Taj Mahal shows the officers' quarters' area. Shrubs were attractively placed around buildings and along the streets. The trees were not large enough to provide protection from the Texas sun. In the foreground was the Commanding General's Quarters, the largest single-family dwelling on Randolph. Beyond it was the Officers' Club, and in the distance was the cadet area.

Designed by San Antonio architect Herbert S. Green, the Commanding General's Quarters cost a hefty $25,000. The quarters featured a two-story living room with exposed rafters and an overlooking balcony. On the ground floor were two bedrooms, two baths, a dining room, a breakfast room, a study, two screened porches, a kitchen, and maids' quarters. Upstairs were two bedrooms and two baths. The AETC commander still lives in this house today.

This was the rear view of the Commanding General's Quarters. The back yard was walled off to provide an informal entertainment area. A two-car garage was to the left. That is the dome of the Taj Mahal peeking over the rooftop.

This was one of the four basic officers' quarters designs, this one for field grade officers (majors and above). It featured a living room, dining room, kitchen, three bedrooms, maid's room (or extra bedroom), and three bathrooms. There was a covered terrace in front and a large porch in the rear. This particular house, labeled as "Bldg No. 12," is now Building 316, located at 3 Military Plaza across from the Officers' Club.

Another option was this one-and-a-half-story company grade officers' quarters. It featured a living room, dining room, kitchen, three bedrooms, maid's room, and three bathrooms. There was a covered patio at the rear and a small porch in front. This particular house, originally Building 271, is now Building 373 at 13 Outer Octagon. The author's future wife lived here as a dependent from 1965 to 1971.

This was the living room of a one-and-a-half-story company grade officers' quarters.

A third option was this two-story company grade officers' quarters, which came in two styles, one with a flat front facade, as pictured here, and another with a slight frontal projection. It had a living room, dining room, kitchen, three bedrooms, maid's room, three bathrooms, a small front porch, and a large, covered rear porch. This was originally Building 163, but is now Building 404, at 3 Northwest Road.

Although this appeared to be a different two-story company grade officers' quarters, it was in fact the same floor plan as the other two-story house style, except the covered porch had been moved to the front of the building. Otherwise, the interior was the same: a living room, separate dining room, kitchen, three bedrooms, maid's room, and three bathrooms. This was Building 142, later renumbered Building 431, at 9 North Park.

Field grade officers had an option besides the one-story quarters. This two-story house featured, on the first floor, a family room, living room, separate dining room, kitchen, maid's room, and a bath. Upstairs were four bedrooms and two baths. This was originally Building 286, later redesignated as Building 312, at 4 North Park. Other than the general's house, this was the largest quarters available.

This was a living room in a company grade officer's house. That is a radio standing in the corner, not a liquor cabinet.

This was one of the many 10-car garages scattered around Randolph. They were nothing more than rectangular, walled enclosures with openings at one end for automobiles and smaller openings at the other for foot traffic. This particular garage still exists as Building 319, on Inner Octagon between Northeast Road and East Park.

This building was typical of the 68 two-story married NCO duplexes built at an average cost of $12,750 each in 1931. Each duplex featured a living room, dining room, and kitchen on the first floor, and four bedrooms (one labeled a "sleeping porch") and a bathroom on the second floor. Today, this building, at 13 H Street East, serves as a transient living facility for Randolph Inn lodging.

There were six enlisted men's barracks on Randolph, and five were for 250 men each. The first floor had rooms for unmarried NCOs, offices for the first sergeant and commanding officer, a mess hall and kitchen, and a dayroom. The second floor had two open-bay squad rooms for 194 men, more NCO rooms, a barbershop, and a tailor shop. Currently, this building is home to the Air Force Recruiting Service.

Building 3 (now Building 499) was the only 300-man enlisted barracks on Randolph. When the initial elements of the Air Force's military personnel function at the Pentagon moved to Randolph in 1963, they occupied various buildings around the base. Building 499 was connected with Building 496 to make one large complex, which opened as the Military Personnel Center in July 1965. Today, it still houses the Air Force Personnel Center.

"Your home away from home" rings hollow when looking at this interior shot of one of the enlisted barracks. This photograph, obviously taken before the barracks were occupied, shows how they were open-bay on the second floor, with no privacy. Soon, the barracks would be filled with cots, footlockers, and other authorized furniture.

This was the mess hall of the 11th Air Base Group's barracks (now Building 499, home of the Air Force Personnel Center) at Christmas in 1938. Even the decorations could not do much for the sparseness of the interior; however, at the end of the Great Depression, these facilities were probably much better than what many of the troops could expect back home.

Even the kitchens of the enlisted barracks were spartan. Here was the Headquarters Squadron kitchen in Building 4, which was later Building 494 and is now merged into Building 499 of the Air Force Personnel Center. This area, too, is now office space.

There were two enlisted men's swimming pools, cannily labeled as "Auxiliary Water Storage Tanks" (probably to escape Congressional criticism of the Air Corps constructing a "country club"). This pool was on the west side. It lasted into the 1990s, when it was filled in because of maintenance problems. The space is now occupied by a new building for the Air Force Personnel Center. The east pool was razed in the 1980s.

This rock garden, waterfall, and pool were located near the Station Hospital (upper left). It probably was not fed from an artesian well, so the water was most likely piped into the pool and pumped to the top of the rocks. The rock garden and pool were located in a triangle of land on Main Circle, about halfway between the Station Hospital and the cadet area. It no longer exists.

There was a second phase in construction on Randolph. In 1933, construction began on the Post Chapel. Funding problems delayed the beginning of this project.

A few months later, the Post Chapel was beginning to take form.

By 1934, the Post Chapel was complete and ready for services. Dedication ceremonies were held on September 2, 1934. A symbolic key to the building was presented to Maj. Gen. Johnson Hagood, then the 8th Corps area commander, who then passed it to Alva J. Brusted, the chief chaplain. Although large, the key actually fit the chapel door.

The Post Chapel, laid out in the shape of a Cross of Lorraine, was modeled after San Antonio's Mission Concepción and Mission San Jose and cost $66,000 to construct. The chapel's right tower had no cupola, reflecting the Spanish custom of leaving a building incomplete. Under Spanish colonial law, an incomplete building was exempt from taxation.

The interior of the Post Chapel was somewhat plain, as one would expect on an Army installation. Later, six stained-glass windows were added, honoring Maj. Gen. Frank P. Lahm, Maj. Gen. Augustine Warner Robins, Aviation Medical Examiners Class 42-F, graduates of the San Antonio Aviation Cadet Center who died during World War II, instructor pilots who died while serving, and deceased enlisted personnel.

Upon completion of the Post Chapel in 1934, the area around Washington Circle was set. This photograph, probably taken in the late 1930s, shows that the landscaping was starting to mask the starkness of Randolph Field, which sprang up from virtually treeless farmland.

Also in the second construction phase were 16 additional NCO duplexes in the southeast corner of the base. This January 4, 1934, photograph shows the foundations of 14 of those duplexes (two others were just out of frame at upper right). The duplexes were completed in 1934. In the foreground was Grater Field. In the triangle of land just above the NCO quarters was the Post School.

In the mid-1930s, relatives of Captain Randolph visited Randolph Field. In this photograph, they are standing on the front steps of the Taj Mahal. Most notably, in the front row at left was Brig. Gen. James E. Chaney, the commander of Air Corps Training Center. In the center are J.D. Randolph (father) and Minnie Randolph (mother).

The Daughters of the American Revolution dedicated a memorial following the planting of 120 live oak trees on Randolph Field in 1932 in celebration of the George Washington bicentennial. Many of these trees still exist on Washington Circle, around the Taj Mahal, North Park, Military Circle, and South Park. This memorial, consisting of native red granite boulders and a bronze tablet, was unveiled on July 3, 1935.

It was not all work and no play for personnel stationed at Randolph Field. Here, some polo players are lined up for the dedication of the new polo grounds on May 19, 1937. The wide-open spaces around Randolph were suitable for such sports.

The QM paint storage building was located just east of the Engine Test Building and north of the Guard House. Built in 1938, it was later expanded by half again. This little, unassuming building was later razed, and its passing was hardly noted.

Maj. Gen. Frank P. Lahm reviewed the Aviation Cadet Regiment on the occasion of his retirement on November 30, 1941, at Randolph Field. Behind him are, from left to right, Lt. Gen. Walter Krueger (obscured), Maj. Gen. Henry V. Strong, Brig. Gen. Martin F. Scanlon, Brig. Gen. Clarence L. Tinker, and Brig. Gen. Hubert R. Harmon.

The Aeromedical Research Laboratory, the last permanent building begun on Randolph before World War II, was finished in 1942. The architectural firm of Phelps, Dewees & Simmons designed the building, which featured an impressive two-story, rounded-arched entrance. Since the School of Aviation Medicine relocated back to Brooks in 1959, the building has hosted a variety of offices over the years, including the 19th Air Force headquarters from 1993 to 2012.

This was how Randolph Field looked on the eve of America's entry into World War II. Although the chapel and some smaller buildings were added during the 1930s, the only other significant additions were the two new cadet barracks (top center), finished in 1939, and the Aeromedical Research Laboratory (not yet constructed at the time of this photograph, which dates it between 1939 and 1941). Within three years, scores of "temporary" buildings, many of which were still there in 1970 when the author first arrived, were crammed into virtually every open area.

Four

AVIATION CADETS

In September 1941, Col. Idwal H. Edwards, commander of Randolph Field, presented regimental colors to the Aviation Cadet Wing. This dramatic photograph caught the spirit and patriotism of the cadets just before America's entry into World War II.

On a wet day, new flying cadets reported to the Taj Mahal for in-processing. There was no consolidated basic training in those days. All training from day one began at the airfield concerned, and if one was an aviation cadet, that meant Randolph Field.

One of the things that had to be done was to get the all-important identification card. In this photograph, cadets were lined up in front of the machine that took the pictures. Note that some of the cadets were half-dressed, wearing only the upper part of their uniform.

Another stop in the cadet in-processing was to get fitted for a uniform. There was a joke in the military that uniforms came in two sizes: too big and too small. In this 1935 photograph, however, it looks like the cadets were getting measured for some well-fitting duds.

Under the watchful eye of an upperclassman, these happy souls left the Cadet Administration Building in March 1933 with duffle bags of gear that they would use in their training. There appear to be the remnants of a snowfall along the walkway.

The old adage "hurry up and wait" comes to mind in this photograph of cadets, both in and out of uniform, reporting to an Air Corps officer. The third cadet in line seemed to be more worried than the others for some reason.

Part of the cadets' training was to learn about parts of the airplane, including armament. In this 1933 photograph, cadets are stripping down what appear to be .30-caliber machine guns.

This was the Academic Department's Radial Engine Section, where student pilots were instructed in the operation and maintenance of the engines that powered the airplanes they flew.

Another part of the cadets' ground training was understanding the intricacies of the engines that propelled the airplanes they would fly. Here, in one of the hangars, cadets examined the ignition system of an aircraft engine. In the left foreground is the crankshaft of an inline, water-cooled engine.

Since they would be flying biplanes, it was important for cadets to learn how to properly rig one. Rigging used wires to properly align both wings with each other and with the proper dihedral to ensure safe operation of the plane. In this photograph, cadets are watching a master mechanic rig the wings of a Boeing PW-9D. The "PW" designation denoted "Pursuit–Water-Cooled."

"Hit a brace, mister! Suck in that gut! Tuck in that chin! I wanna see some wrinkles!" In this photograph, a "dodo" (new cadet) received instructions from an upperclassman. From the looks of the cadet's armpit, it was either a hot day or he had been taking a lot of "heat" from the upperclassmen.

An essential part of the cadets' ground training was "flying" the ubiquitous Link Trainer. Not only was it economical, it also avoided future accidents by properly preparing novice flyers for the flying experience and by eliminating those who had no aptitude for aviating. Introduced in the mid-1930s, this pioneer device used pumps, valves, and bellows to simulate the motion of flight through all three axes. Also, there were basic instruments inside that accustomed the cadets to understanding how they were to be used. A nearby instructor's station was a desk with a map and a set of instruments that duplicated what was showing inside the trainer. A device tracked across the map and showed the cadet's progress in "flying" a pattern. Headphones and microphones connected instructor to student. The hood over the trainer could be lowered to teach instrument flying.

"I did it!" could be the cry from this happy cadet as he and his friends celebrate a successful flight in the Link Trainer. Over 500,000 US pilots were schooled in Link Trainers from the 1930s to the 1950s. During the war, Link churned out over 10,000 "Blue Boxes."

This photograph brings to mind the quote attributed to the Duke of Wellington: "The Battle of Waterloo was won on the playing fields of Eton." Cadets received fencing instruction while at Randolph. This honed reflexes and developed a sharp eye that would be essential to survival in the skies over Europe and the Pacific.

Physical fitness was an essential part of a cadet's training. Here is a group of cadets undergoing calisthenics on the grounds in front of Barracks B. In the near future, a new barracks would be built behind the cadets that would not allow occupants of the NCO duplexes in the background to see what was going on in the cadet grounds.

The first phase of cadet flying training was primary. Before their first flights, cadets received their parachutes.

In this photograph, a cadet receives some last-minute advice from his instructor before climbing into his Consolidated PT-3, nicknamed "Trusty." These low-powered trainers introduced fledgling pilots to the experience of flying without unduly challenging their skills.

An instructor and his student prepare to take up their Stearman PT-13A "Kaydet" on the west flight line. They appear to be using a Gosport speaking tube to communicate. Gosports used acoustics rather than electrically transmitted sound.

Here, a cadet prepares for some blind flying in a North American BT-9. Blind flying required cadets to rely on just their instruments to navigate their planes. An instructor flew along in case the cadet was heading for trouble.

Back on the ground, pilots used a model North American BT-9 to discuss the day's flying.

There are 11 guys in this photograph, but it was not a football huddle. It was just an attempt by the photographer to capture the exuberance of the cadet flyers at Randolph at the beginning of World War II.

No, this was not a flock of penguins that wandered onto Randolph's east ramp. These flying cadets displayed their seat pack parachutes as they waddled out to their North American BT-9s.

It looks like some cadet hijinks are occurring here. The "pilot" was pulling back on the stick, trying to gain altitude for his crewmates.

Determination and enthusiasm were reflected in the faces of these aviation cadets as they marched past their North American BT-14s on Randolph's east flight line. BT-14s differed from BT-9s in that they had longer, all-metal fuselages instead of fabric-covered ones, straight trailing edge rudders, and slightly larger engines. Many of these cadets would go on to Kelly Field to fly North American AT-6s.

Military training was part of a cadet's life. This included inspections and drill. In this 1936 photograph, an Air Corps officer points out a discrepancy to an aviation cadet during a white-glove inspection. This scene took place in a room in one of the two aviation cadet barracks at the time. Everything was expected to be in its proper place, including items in the drawers.

In this photograph, the cadet wing stood at attention on the parade grounds south of the NCO duplexes on the west side of Randolph. The cadet area was at the top of the photograph. This was taken after 1939, because the two newest barracks were already built.

With the band keeping time with a military march, cadet units passed in review on the parade grounds on the southwest side of Randolph Field.

Although the original caption on this 1932 photograph said that these cadets were "passing in review," it is more likely that they were just drilling in front of one of the dorms and practicing "eyes right."

The cadet drum and bugle corps performed in the circle between the Academic Building and the Cadet Administration Building.

"March, march, march, that's all we do is march!" This nicely framed photograph shows cadets marching from Cadet Barracks A to the Cadet Administration Building, mostly likely for chow.

There was nothing like a little close-order drill with some Springfield rifles and pistol belts to whet appetites for chow. The cadet at right wore a Sam Browne belt, which not only looked sharp but also held the scabbard for the saber he was carrying in his right hand.

This scene from Metro-Goldwyn-Mayer's 1935 film *West Point of the Air* shows three identifiable actors. Under the letter A is Robert Young, B is Wallace Beery, and C is Lewis Stone. There would be two more movies filmed at Randolph: *I Wanted Wings* (1941) and *Air Cadet* (1951). It is difficult to be sure, but the airplane behind Young appears to be a Douglas BT-2B.

In this scene from *West Point of the Air*, cadets are introduced to an early Link Trainer. Second from the left is Robert Young, and a youthful Robert Taylor sits in the trainer. Also in the movie were Maureen O'Sullivan, Rosalind Russell, and James Gleason.

Consolidated PT-3As warmed up on the west ramp in preparation for a mass takeoff for the cameras filming *West Point of the Air*. Movies about the armed forces were popular during the Great Depression years.

This photograph is unique because it not only features a flyover of biplanes in formation spelling "USA," but also because it shows the rarely photographed rear of the Taj Mahal, which featured the entrance to the movie theater.

Five

Randolph Field Aircraft

In this dramatic night photograph, a North American BT-14 pilot receives last-minute instructions prior to takeoff for some night flying.

The Consolidated PT-3 was used at Randolph Field from the beginning of operations in November 1931. Here, 1st Lt. C.T. Mower has the engine running and is preparing to leave the west flying field.

A 53rd School Squadron mechanic stands beside his PT-3 with toolbox open and engine uncowled, ready for inspection.

This 1939 photograph shows the older PT-3s lined up on the west flight ramp, with newer Stearman PT-13s in the distance. Note how the span of the wings changes about one-third of the way down the middle row.

According to the label on this 1933 photograph, "Capt Easterbrook" was flying this Consolidated PT-11. Generally speaking, the PT-11 was about the same size as its predecessor, the PT-3, but featured curved outlines and better streamlining.

Consolidated PT-11s and their mechanics of the 53rd School Squadron await inspection in this July 8, 1933, photograph. Note the drip pans under the engines; one had to keep the hangar floor clean.

A Consolidated PT-11D sits on the west ramp of Randolph Field in May 1937.

A PT-13 cruises near Randolph Field in January 1937. The PT-13 and its close cousin the PT-17 would serve well into World War II, giving thousands of pilots their first taste of flying.

A PT-13 does a banking turn over Randolph Field in this May 1938 photograph. The road that led north out of the field and across the railroad tracks and then bent to the left was State Highway 218, better known as Pat Booker Road today. Built in 1935 to connect Randolph with State Highway 2 (later US Highway 81, then Interstate 35), it enabled Randolph personnel to quickly connect with Fort Sam Houston, Brooks Field, and Kelly Field. Francis P. "Pat" Booker was a popular officer who was assigned to Randolph and then transferred to Maxwell Field, Alabama. While there, he was killed in an aircraft accident in September 1936. A San Antonio native, he was buried at Fort Sam Houston National Cemetery. Randolph officials persuaded the State of Texas to name Highway 218 after Captain Booker.

A six-ship formation of Randolph PT-13As flies over the stark West Texas landscape on May 10, 1938. Except for a few roads, scattered farms, and creek beds, one area of this part of Texas looked just like another, which must have been a challenge to the fledgling pilots, just as it is when trying to identify where this photograph was taken.

PT-13s stand ready for flight on the west flight line in this 1938 photograph.

The Douglas BT-1 was one of the last Air Corps airplanes to use the famous World War I Liberty engine. Here, a BT-1 and its faithful mechanic are ready for inspection. BT-1s were phased out in 1935.

Douglas BT-1s flank officers and enlisted men in this July 8, 1933, inspection of the 52nd School Squadron. Three of the officers in the photograph are Maj. Frederick L. Martin, commander of Randolph Field (far left); E.D. Jones; and Oakley G. Kelly. Kelly flew an Air Service Fokker T-2 transport plane on the first nonstop coast-to-coast flight in May 1923.

The Douglas BT-2B was one of the initial basic trainers used at Randolph when operations began in November 1931. The design of the BT-2B was derived from the Douglas O-32, an observation plane from the late 1920s.

This line crew poses with a Douglas BT-2B as it is refueled on an apron in front of Hangar K on the east flight line.

No, this was not a Douglas BT-2B riddled with antiaircraft fire by accident during a training exercise. Rather, it was an airplane ready for inspection, with all of its access panels (some metal, some fabric) open and its mechanic standing by to the left of the engine.

These Douglas BT-2Bs wait on the east flight line for student pilots in 1934.

A rare plane indeed was Randolph's Consolidated BT-6, seen here winging over the Texas landscape. Originally a YPT-11, it was fitted with a more powerful 300-horsepower Wright J-6 engine and given the BT-6 designation. Only one was built. It was not unusual for Depression-era manufacturers to "stretch" a design into other uses with engine changes, in the hopes of securing additional contracts.

Another rare bird was Randolph's Consolidated Y1BT-7. The "Y" designation stood for "service test," and the "1" indicated that it was procured from additional funds rather than fiscal year funds. Starting out as Y1PT-12s, a small group of just 10 planes were given more powerful 300-horsepower Pratt & Whitney Wasp Junior R-985A engines and subsequently redesignated as BT-7s.

The Seversky BT-8 had two claims to fame. First, it was the first Army basic trainer specifically built to be a trainer, rather than a rehash of an observation plane or a primary trainer on steroids. Second, it was the first Air Corps production monoplane trainer. Due to the fact that it was somewhat expensive, tricky to fly, and difficult to maintain, the BT-8 was soon eclipsed by the North American BT-9.

A new basic training airplane arrived at Randolph in 1936, the North American BT-9. A monoplane with fixed landing gear, this airplane would be improved over the next few years, leading to the BT-14 and then to the famous AT-6 "Texan."

by June 1939, the east flight line had over 100 BT-9s lined up. Note that the field, except for the aprons in front of the hangars, was still grass.

No pre–World War II photographic essay would be complete without an image of Air Corps airplanes flying in echelon. These North American BT-9s are holding a reasonable formation.

The old Army Air Corps loved inspections. Here, a bevy of BT-9s and their anxious mechanics await the critical eyes of the inspectors inside a Randolph hangar.

It is unclear why these North American BT-9s are in such a jumble. Housecleaning, perhaps? Parking the planes this close together and in different directions meant that the mechanics pushed them into these positions.

Pilots walk toward their waiting North American BT-9s on the east ramp of Randolph. In the distance is the neighboring town of Schertz.

This is a nice photograph of a North American BT-9 winging over the officers' quarters area of Randolph.

A nice, fluffy cloud provides a backdrop for this North American BT-14. North American Aviation eventually built 251 BT-14s, with the lion's share of them coming to Randolph Field. These trainers used 450-horsepower Pratt & Whitney R-985-25 engines, which were later downgraded to 400-horsepower R-985-11s.

Here, on the east flight line, an instructor points out details of the North American BT-14 to a group of attentive aviation cadets.

This Curtis P-6E Hawk, flown by Lt. G.F. Schlatter from the 17th Pursuit Squadron at Selfridge Field, Michigan, was a visitor to Randolph Field in 1933. The P-6E shared first-line pursuit duties with the more agile Boeing P-12 in the Army Air Corps during the early 1930s.

Brig. Gen. Charles H. Danforth, commander of the Air Corps Training Center, needed a personal aircraft. Instead of using some underpowered training plane to get around, his steed was the Boeing P-12E, a first-line pursuit plane at the time. An Air Corps photographer took this picture at Randolph on November 10, 1932.

Just passing through Randolph Field in November 1933 was this National Guard Douglas O-38E observation plane from the 116th Observation Squadron at Felts Field, Washington.

This photograph serves as an appropriate closing to this book. When the United States entered World War II, it had already begun to ramp up its flying training program to provide pilots for the thousands of airplanes that were going to be built. Randolph Field had to expand quickly, so there was no time for permanent buildings. Instead, many temporary buildings were constructed and placed in unused areas of the base. This photograph, taken late in the war or just after, shows how the buildings were sited on the airfield. In the foreground, nascent Universal City, still unincorporated, had gained a block of 14 temporary buildings, the Civilian War Housing Project, built next to the railroad tracks to accommodate civilians working at Randolph. Note also that concrete runways, including a diagonal runway, had been added. Additionally, a south ramp with two large hangers had been built in 1945 for Boeing B-29 "Superfortress" training that abruptly terminated with the surrender of Japan.